THE OPTIONS TRADER'S BIBLE
MASTER THE MARKETS
UTILIZING OPTIONS CONTRACTS

KYLE J

FOUNDER OF OPINICUS HOLDINGS,
THE #1 OPTIONS TRADING EDUCATION PROVIDER

ACKNOWLEDGMENTS

Dedicated to my father,
who taught me the value of hard work, staying persistent,
and having unwavering confidence.
Also, for sparking my interest in the stock market
when I was at the young age of 14.

Special thanks to friends and family who assisted in the creation of this book.

Additionally, an applause to all of the traders within the Opinicus group who encourage, motivate, and hold one another accountable through thick and thin. Teaching others about options trading has been a phenomenal adventure for me so far. I am thankful and owe a significant debt of appreciation to the students and trading enthusiasts that I have had the pleasure of trading side by side with. The countless messages I receive about changing people's perception of the market and trading acumen is what continuously pushes me forward in this space.

FOREWORD

My goal as the creator of Opinicus Holdings, and as the author of *The Options Traders Bible* has been to give folks the necessary knowledge and confidence to engage with the financial markets with detailed understanding, and come away with profits. Producing profit from your own trades brings a feeling that no adviser or money manager can provide. This brutally honest book will provide you with the know-how needed to excel with options trading.

The messages found within are built upon my very own real world experiences; not those of hedge fund managers or institutional investors with unrealistic and seemingly endless bank rolls. While options trading is a challenge to master: You can do it, and trust me it will take plenty of work - But it is certainly realistic. The road to becoming a successful options trader has no shortcuts or back roads, despite what many are claiming. You will face various hurdles, many of them emotional. With the detailed direction presented in this book, the risk management I encourage, and the discipline I promote, these hurdles will be minor speed bumps on your journey.

Now, I present to you a comprehensive roadmap that I am happy to share. Prepare yourself for elevated levels of discipline and trading acumen that you have not previously reached!

INTRODUCTION

Become one of the successful few who place stone upon stone until they have a solid foundation of knowledge and experience that will last them all their lives. You cannot go into any endeavor and make money or become prominent just like that—you must serve your apprenticeship.

The perfect strategy when it comes to trading in general, and specifically options trading, is like the Holy Grail. It doesn't exist, and the people looking for it (or paying hard-earned money for it) are wasting their time and money chasing a fairy tale!

That being said, there certainly are strategies, methods, and procedures that are superior to others, particularly for the retail trader.

> *It is not so much your strategy, but your unequivocal willingness to obey your rules and follow your risk management policy.*

Unfortunately in today's environment, we have many "pros" and "gurus" who speak of having the (nonexistent) holy strategy; naturally, it costs hundreds if not thousands of dollars. While the self-proclaimed pro or guru may have spent a fair amount of time compiling somewhat relevant information, they usually have no real experience in the field of swing trading and day trading. So their information is superficial at best! Remember, there is a huge difference between teaching from theory and teaching from experience. There are a lot of people presenting themselves as experts who haven't executed a single trade.

That leaves us with the amateur trader thinking they have the knowledge necessary to begin trading. In reality, this new trader is left with a massive void, one that should be filled by the most important concept in trading: RISK MANAGEMENT. Unfortunately, I have heard the tale time and time again of the unprepared amateur, and have even witnessed their struggles firsthand.

Take a deep breath: Mastering your mind, and thus your emotions, is the most challenging part of trading. Fortunately for you, this book will help you through the process, which took me years (and thousands of dollars in losses) to master.

Options: What are they?

Now, if you're reading this, you likely already understand what options contracts on the stock market are. However, I am going to assume that you do not, and upon my promise of a comprehensive guide, will be covering all the bases here.

An options contract, by definition, is the right but not the obligation to purchase underlying shares at a later date (expiration) at a predetermined price (strike). They are an agreement between you and another individual, with the broker acting as the "middle man" to guarantee the contract. This definition will become clearer as the book progresses.

There are two types of options contracts: call and put. To describe this simply, calls equate to buying (going long on) a stock; puts equate to selling (going short on) a stock. Puts and calls can be found within your broker's options chain. The options chain contains all the different options available to be purchased.

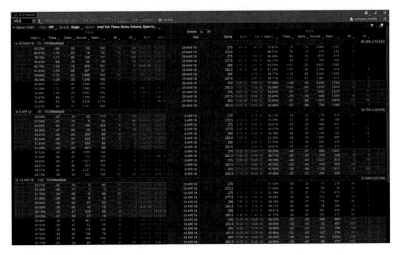

Typical options chain: Calls on the left, puts on the right, with expiration and strike in the middle. Image courtesy of TDAmeritrade.

Why trade options?

Simply put, options trades have a roughly 33% probability of winning. The underlying stock price action can be flat, up, or down. We increase our probability of winning using specific strategies, which will be outlined in this book. Options can be used to reduce the overall cost of trading, as compared to trading only stocks. Options are also leveraged, meaning a small move in the underlying stock could result in a big move for your options contract.

Options are the best form of income generation investment on the stock market. From big bankrolls to small, there is something for everyone. With smart risk management procedures in place, a strong desire to increase portfolio size, and proper guidance, anyone can increase their portfolio size using options.

MONEY & RISK MANAGEMENT

As previously mentioned, this is, hands-down, the most important topic when it comes to actively trading and managing your own positions. It all boils down to the simple concept of risk versus reward. This topic (or rather the neglect of) is a large reason why some traders fail; developing and sticking to a philosophy is the backbone of every successful trading career. It is the number one concept in trading that must be mastered.

Follow your rules objectively and
PROTECT your capital without question.

Remind yourself—often—that losses will occur. This is part of being a trader, and it is a daily occurrence for some. The goal is to consistently make more than you lose. Anyone who tells you they have a 100% (or close to) win rate is lying!

People lose in the markets for a number of reasons. Most commonly, they don't have a plan (RULES!) before making a trade: they let their losers run and cut their winners short, and they go "all-in" out of desperation to try to recoup some losses. The root of this cycle that plagues so many new traders is emotion. This type of trader becomes emotionally tied to the money they have lost and goes into a bit of a panic when things don't go as they want. Unfortunately, the trader at this point has likely already experienced substantial devastation to their account. How can we avoid this?

The dominoes are your portfolio. The person is your risk management policy.

The top characteristics of a great performing trader are easy to define and recognize, but much more challenging to emulate. Profitable traders can be described as cool, calm, and collected—which results in them being emotionless during the period of the day when they are trading. This, in turn, means they always respect their rules!

> *You can't win the war against the markets if*
> *you can't win the war against your own mind.*

Having a good grasp on the technical moves and psychology of price action is essential not only to your risk management procedure, but to your trading plan as well. We will dive into these topics in later chapters.

Baseline rules to follow

Remember: your biggest losses come when you do not respect your trading plan (rules). The rules I have always recommended to new members of the Opinicus trading group are as follows:

- Never lose more than 5% of your account in any one (losing) trade. Calculate position size accordingly.
  o Example: With an account of about $5k, you'd take a $250 max risk on any one trade.
- Use 5%-10% of your account per trade with a stop-loss of 10%-15% on the position.
- Be at least 50% correct in the direction of your trades, with a reward-risk ratio of 2.5:1.
- Identify where you could be wrong and what will happen if you're wrong before entering into a trade.
- Always capture 25% optimal gain when possible UNLESS the position is running hard at the moment of truth.
- Always trade the same dollar amount per play. That way, if you win 6 out of 10 plays you're still a winner.

This basic risk management procedure has made countless students and traders within our group wildly successful. Of course, as your skills advance, you can tweak the system to your liking, but this is a great core set of rules.

OPTIONS GREEKS

When you open your options chain with your broker, you'll likely see columns for theta, delta, gamma, and vega—collectively known as the options Greeks. Understanding the Greeks is essential to understanding changes in options contract prices overtime. The values of the Greeks are derived from complex mathematical equations. These equations have no relevance to your profitability with trading. You can trust that the values provided by your broker are accurate. While they may seem confusing at first, as we progress through the material of this book, they will become increasingly clear.

Theta

Theta is very important for determining what expiration date to select for your option. Theta is most simply defined as the time decay of your option contract: for each day that passes, the option's value will decline by the amount of theta.

This options chain for $LMT shows the Greeks.

For example, in photo above we see that the 325 strike calls have a theta of -.27 and a bid price of 1.45 with an ask price of 1.60. If you purchase the 325 calls at 1.60 and decide to hold the option overnight, that contract would lose .27 of value, assuming all other conditions held constant. This means that it would be down to 1.33 the next day. That is a significant loss of 16%! Clearly, this would not be a wise trade to take.

This being said, if you plan to hold an options position for any amount of time, you need to be very particular with your expiration date. It is in your best interest to get a low theta value on your position.

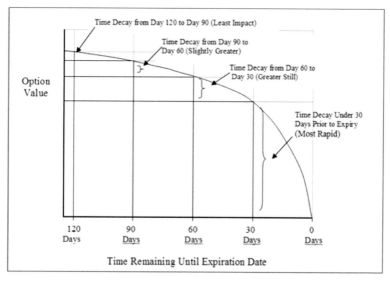

Theta time decay and how it accelerates.

Of course, there are scenarios where having a high theta value is not a problem. If you plan on holding a particular position only for an intraday move, then expiration in the same week or the following week is fine. If you intend to hold a position for a few days, then you will want an expiration that is at least two to three weeks out.

Option chain showing Greeks. As you can see, theta values decrease as you look at contracts with longer-term expirations.

Delta

Delta is a fairly simply options metric. It can be defined as how much the option price will move relative to a $1 move in the underlying stock. It can also be referred to as a percentage of the underlying $1 move.

Here is an example: Looking at the option chain in the figure below, we can see that the delta for the 305 strike calls is .51. The bid price is 10.90 and the ask price is 11.30. At the time of this example, $TSLA was trading at 303. Within an hour, $TSLA moved up to 304. What happened to the price of our 305 strike calls? Being that the delta value is .51, our option contract value increased by 0.51! That means that the bid would now be 11.41 and the ask would be 11.81.

So, for each $1 move in the underlying, we look to delta to determine how our option contract will be affected. As you can see on the option chain, delta values are not held constant for all strike prices. I personally enjoy purchasing options contracts that have a delta value of 0.30 or higher. With a higher delta value, you get more gain on your options contracts for a smaller move in the underlying price.

		CALLS				Strikes: 14			PUTS				
Delta	Gamma	Theta	Vega	Bid X	Ask X	Exp	Strike	Bid X	Ask X	Delta	Gamma	Theta	Vega
4 MAY 18	(2) 100(Weeklys)												109.80% (±23.473)
.74	.01	-1.82	.08	21.90 A	22.20 X	4 MAY 18	287.5	1.05 Z	1.10 X	.26	.01	-1.58	.09
.71	.01	-1.70	.09	20.05 B	20.55 X	4 MAY 18	290	1.65 D	1.95 X	.29	.01	-1.61	.09
.68	.01	-1.77	.10	18.25 X	18.90 X	4 MAY 18	292.5	1.45 X	1.70 H	.32	.01	-1.67	.10
.65	.01	-1.82	.10	16.75 X	17.20 X	4 MAY 18	295	2.35 X	2.70 X	.35	.01	-1.71	.10
.62	.01	-1.87	.11	15.20 A	15.70 A	4 MAY 18	297.5	6.15 Z	6.50 X	.38	.01	-1.74	.11
.59	.01	-1.89	.11	13.75 Z	14.10 B	4 MAY 18	300	9.25 X	9.50 F	.42	.01	-1.76	.11
.56	.01	-1.90	.11	12.30 Z	12.75 X	4 MAY 18	302.5	11.30 Z	11.55 XB	.45	.01	-1.76	.11
.51	.01	-1.68	.11	10.90 X	11.30 Z	4 MAY 18	305	14.25 M	13.75 BP	.49	.01	-1.75	.11
.48	.01	-1.86	.11	9.50 X	10.00 Z	4 MAY 18	307.5	12.80 X	12.90 X	.52	.01	-1.72	.11
.44	.01	-1.32	.11	8.45 X	9.30 X	4 MAY 18	310	13.80 X	14.25 X	.56	.01	-1.68	.11
.40	.01	-1.76	.11	7.35 X	7.65 Z	4 MAY 18	312.5	15.25 Z	15.60 Z	.59	.01	-1.61	.11
.37	.01	-1.70	.10	6.40 Z	6.65 X	4 MAY 18	315	16.80 Y	19.70 VA	.63	.01	-1.58	.10
.33	.01	-1.61	.10	5.45 A	5.70 A	4 MAY 18	317.5	18.25 F	19.05 TA	.66	.01	-1.55	.10
.30	.01	-1.50	.10	4.55 M	4.80 Q	4 MAY 18	320	19.95 Q	20.40 Z	.70	.01	-1.45	.10

This screen shows the option chain for $TSLA.

Gamma

Gamma, much like delta, relies on the underlying stock price action to move $1. Gamma is the movement of delta if the share price moves $1.

Using the same $TSLA option chain from the previous example, we can see that the gamma for the 305 strike calls is .01. So, using the same example as before, we assume $TSLA is trading at 303, and over the next hour makes its way to 304. What does this do to the value of delta? Moves it up by .01 from .51 to .52.

Knowledge of how gamma works is essential to having a well-rounded options education; but gamma does not need to play a big role in your trading.

Vega

Vega is something I personally never look at, but you may be interested to know what it is. Vega can be defined as how the option price will move relative to a 1% move of implied volatility. We have not yet gone over implied volatility (IV). When we do, vega will become clear.

OPTIONS BASICS

There are a handful of options metrics that are essential to your knowledge as a trader. You will use these, or at least refer to them, with every single options trade that you place.

Implied volatility

This is arguably one of the most important metrics for options traders. What is implied volatility (IV)? IV is a mathematical calculation based upon standard deviation. However, as with the Greeks, knowledge of this calculation is not essential to turning a profit with options.

IV is most often explained as a prediction of how volatile the option is going to be. If IV goes up, it can be referred to as a "premium spike." IV is a great tool for determining how cheap or expensive your option contract is.

IV is shown in the far-left column of this options chain.

For example, when you purchase an option with high IV, and IV comes down (whether it be over a few minutes, hours, or days), you will lose value on your option contract even if the price of the underlying does not dip! What might cause IV to spike? Characteristically it spikes around big events—specifically earnings reports, geopolitical events, federal reserve meetings, and the like.

I tend to stay away from any IV values that are above 50%. If you are looking at purchasing options with IV values above 50%, you need to know exactly why the stock has these increased levels. This knowledge is essential to your trading plan. IV ties in directly to our next topic.

Options premium

The options premium is what you see when you're looking at the bid/ask spread (the cost of the options contract). It is defined as the price of any specific option that has yet to expire—i.e., the market price. Premium is quoted as the dollar amount per share, and 1 option contract represents 100 shares. For example, if the particular option you are interested in buying has an ask price of 1.50, it would cost you $150 to purchase 1 contract.

Volume

Volume shows you the number of contracts traded (so far) during the day. Volume is extremely important for options trading, because it represents an audience—meaning it will be far easier to exit your trade. Lower volume could indicate that you will struggle to get out of your trade when you have reached your profit target or your stop-loss.

		CALLS			Strikes: 14	
	Volume	Open.Int	Bid X	Ask X	Exp	Strike
11 MAY 18 (3) 100(Weeklys)						
	195	3,274	15.10 X	15.35 X	11 MAY 18	170
	51	3,565	12.60 C	12.95 C	11 MAY 18	172.5
	1,730	5,903	10.15 C	10.40 X	11 MAY 18	175
	599	5,536	7.70 X	7.95 X	11 MAY 18	177.5
	1,845	11,579	5.30 X	5.50 X	11 MAY 18	180
	7,400	6,205	3.20 X	3.30 N	11 MAY 18	182.5
	17,793	13,657	1.58 Z	1.61 P	11 MAY 18	185
	17,515	13,562	.63 X	.67 Q	11 MAY 18	187.5
	12,796	12,945	.23 H	.24 N	11 MAY 18	190
	5,140	7,033	.09 X	.10 Z	11 MAY 18	192.5
	3,273	5,174	.04 X	.06 H	11 MAY 18	195
	1,993	3,917	.03 A	.04 X	11 MAY 18	197.5
	111	5,790	.01 X	.03 M	11 MAY 18	200
	223	2,335	.01 Z	.02 X	11 MAY 18	202.5

This screen of $AAPL calls shows volume, open interest, and bid/ask spread.

Higher volume on options brings the bid/ask values closer together, which is ideal for both trade entry and exit. The Opinicus strategies discussed later in this book focus strictly on options with particularly high volume. Note: Volume can also be referred to as liquidity.

Options expiry

Options expiration (aka options expiry) is the date that the options contract will expire. Expiry is very important to consider when placing your trade. Farther-out expirations will be less volatile but will also be more expensive. You will also experience less time decay on a farther-out expiration contract, as the theta value is lower. Certain stocks and indexes will have various options expiration dates. For example, $SPY, the S&P500 tracking ETF, has multiple weekly expiries, on Monday, Wednesday, and Friday. It also has monthly expiring options contracts as well. However, a majority of equities have only monthly expiring options. Only those with larger volume and popularity have weekly expiring options.

How do you choose the right expiration date? This all depends on your trading plan: If you intend to do an intraday trade, using a same-week or following-week expiry is acceptable. Any plans to hold contracts overnight should be based on an expiry of a minimum of two to three weeks out. Any plans to hold over the weekend or a period of multiple days should be based on an expiry of three to four weeks. We follow a structure like this due to the decay on options contracts, as discussed in the section about options Greeks, specifically theta.

Strike price

Selecting strike price can be overwhelming. We have three zones to choose from when selecting our strike: at the money (ATM), in the money (ITM), and out of the money (OTM). *At the money* refers to the strike price closest to where the underlying is currently trading. *In the money* refers to any contracts below the current price for calls and above the current price for puts. *Out of the money* refers to any contracts above the current price of the underlying for calls and below for puts.

Various strike prices shown for $BIIB. At the time it was trading at $284.

When selecting strike price for a trade, I will generally select an ATM or slightly OTM (by 1 to 2 strikes) price. This selection will allow you to receive the quickest, most explosive gain on your position. Of course, it all comes down to what the trade plan calls for on any particular trade.

TIME FRAMES & CANDLES

Knowing what time frames to utilize in your research when establishing your trade plan is essential. The time frame you use to create your trade plan will determine which expiry you are going to select. All of the time frames discussed below use a candlestick pattern chart, which is ideal for a trader's pattern recognition.

This is a 1-day, 5-minute candlestick pattern chart for $AXP.

Candlestick charts show the open, high, low, and close price for a particular time period. In the above screen, we see a 1-day, 5-minute chart. Each candle represents a period of 5 minutes. All of the candles you see make up the period of 1 trading day—hence, 1-day, 5-minute (1d 5m) chart.

How does a candlestick work? This graphic explains it best:

Candlestick Basics

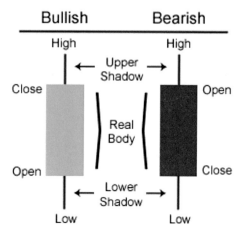

We will not go too in-depth on candles, as I assume this is review for most people who have picked up this book. If it is not, study the graphic to the left, as it has all you need to know about candles. We will get into specific detail about pattern recognition on candlestick charts later.

Now that we understand those basics, what time frames should we use?

Suggested time frames (d = day, m = minute):

- **2d 2m**: Great if you're looking for entry on very quick day trades and morning momentum trades (I will discuss both of these trade types later).
- **2d 3m**: I usually use this time frame to confirm patterns that I am seeing on the 2m chart.
- **5d 5m**: This is the best confirmation pattern for a day trade, and a personal favorite. This chart setup can also be used for analyzing patterns within the past few days, so I occasionally use it for analysis.
- **30d 1h**: An absolutely essential time frame for analysis—your analysis is not complete without a glance at the 1-hour chart.

THE OPTIONS TRADERS BIBLE

- **180d 4h**: Additionally helpful for analysis, this can be used to see after-hours or premarket price action moves that the daily chart won't necessarily show.
- **1y 1d:** Another must-use time frame for analysis. This gives you the best big-picture idea of what price action is doing.

As you can see, smaller time frames are great for executing trades and day trading, while larger time frames are better for overall analysis. Seeing a pattern on a shorter time frame and again on a longer time frame offers strong confirmation that your analysis is correct.

FUNDAMENTAL ANALYSIS

Fundamental analysis is not to be confused with the "analysis" that has been discussed in previous chapters — those are technical analyses, which we will dive into later in this book.

What is fundamental analysis? Fundamental analysis can be described as a method of studying a company's economic and financial factors in order to measure its intrinsic value. Put more simply: If a company is profitable, with good products in the pipeline, and is not overvalued on the stock market presently, then it "should" be a good buy. Of course, this is a generalization. There are a ton of variables that come into play when looking at the fundamentals of a company.

These are the important factors you need to understand when it comes to fundamental analysis:

- **Shares outstanding**: Refers to company stock currently held by ALL shareholders, including shares held by institutions and restricted shares held by officers of the company.
- **Float:** Shares actually available for trading. This includes all shares not presently held by insiders, employees, or other major long-term shareholders.
- **Market capitalization:** Market cap is the market value at a given point in time of the shares outstanding, multiplied by the current share price. Market cap categories are:
  - Mega cap = >200b

- o Large cap = 10-200b
- o Mid cap = 2-10b
- o Small cap = 300m-2b
- o Micro cap = 50m-300m
- o Nano cap = <50m

- **Dilution:** When a company issues additional shares, usually in an effort to raise cash. Generally this is a negative sign, as it signals to investors that the company does not have enough cash reserves.
- **P/E:** Also known as price-to-earnings ratio. Higher P/E indicates that investors are paying a higher price per share compared to its earnings. This is why a lower P/E is better. It tells us that the share price is cheap compared to its earnings.
- **Forward P/E ratio:** The valuation ratio of a company's current share price in comparison to its forecasted earnings per share. This is not as reliable as current P/E ratio. This metric should always be taken with a grain of salt, as it is based on estimates and not actual numbers.
- **Earnings per share (EPS):** Portion of a company's profit allocated to each outstanding share of common stock. This serves as an indicator of a company's profitability.

Those are the basic points of fundamental analysis you'll want to examine. This information is available online from a number of sources (Yahoo Finance, a simple Google search, etc.). My personal favorite source for this kind of information is Finviz.com.

Index	DJIA S&P500	P/E	17.34	EPS (ttm)	10.85	Insider Own	0.06%	Shs Outstand	5.04B	Perf Week	0.44%
Market Cap	948.60B	Forward P/E	14.17	EPS next Y	13.28	Insider Trans	-9.20%	Shs Float	5.04B	Perf Month	5.98%
Income	55.92B	PEG	1.29	EPS next Q	2.18	Inst Own	63.90%	Short Float	1.01%	Perf Quarter	12.43%
Sales	247.42B	P/S	3.83	EPS this Y	10.80%	Inst Trans	-1.00%	Short Ratio	1.51	Perf Half Y	8.17%
Book/sh	25.25	P/B	7.48	EPS next Y	15.62%	ROA	14.30%	Target Price	194.49	Perf Year	21.04%
Cash/sh	17.45	P/C	10.79	EPS next 5Y	13.45%	ROE	40.00%	52W Range	142.20 - 180.37	Perf YTD	11.20%
Dividend	2.92	P/FCF	20.26	EPS past 5Y	7.90%	ROI	18.30%	52W High	-1.95%	Beta	1.29
Dividend %	1.55%	Quick Ratio	1.40	Sales past 5Y	7.90%	Gross Margin	38.30%	52W Low	31.37%	ATR	3.43
Employees	123000	Current Ratio	1.50	Sales Q/Q	15.60%	Oper. Margin	26.70%	RSI (14)	61.96	Volatility	1.12% 1.91%
Optionable	Yes	Debt/Eq	0.96	EPS Q/Q	30.10%	Profit Margin	21.50%	Rel Volume	0.47	Prev Close	188.18
Shortable	Yes	LT Debt/Eq	0.80	Earnings	May 01 AMC	Payout	24.20%	Avg Volume	33.66M	Price	186.66
Recom	2.00	SMA20	5.80%	SMA50	6.88%	SMA200	11.05%	Volume	11,159,184	Change	-0.81%

This screen from Finviz.com shows fundamentals of $AAPL.

Fundamentals can be great for longer-term investing. As this is a book about options trading, I'll tell you that you will not need any information about fundamentals to be profitable as an options trader. That being said, it is still great knowledge to have.

TECHNICAL ANALYSIS

What is it?

Technical analysis (TA) is the study of markets and charts based upon price action and volume only. This form of analysis is what is primarily used by the Opinicus team and myself to profit from the markets. Technical analysis should be used as a guide only—it is not a firm set of rules. When conducting your analysis, always remember to keep things simple: too much analysis can cause paralysis, referred to as analysis paralysis.

Support, resistance, trendlines

These are three of my favorite analysis measures, as most TA yields too much noise and is unnecessary for being profitable in the market. I prefer to take a simplistic approach to looking at price action, as you will see as this book progresses.

Support can be defined as a barrier, zone, or area where a downtrend in price action can be expected to pause.

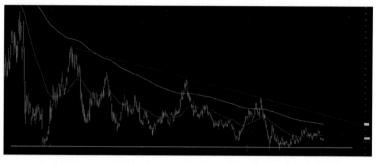

The green line toward the bottom of the $NUGT chart shows support around the 22 level. This is a 3y 1d chart, and as we know, the longer the time frame, the stronger the pattern. So this particular level of support is a very strong one.

As the price of the security (stock) drops, demand for the shares increases, and buyers step in to purchase shares in that support zone. Areas of support are good places to establish a long (calls) entry on a position. One important thing to remember is that when price action pushes through (below) a support level, that support level will often become a resistance level.

Resistance can be defined as a barrier, zone, or area where an uptrend in price action can be expected to pause. As the price of the stock rises, demand for shares begins to decrease, and short interest increases. Remember, when price action pushes through a resistance point, it will often become support.

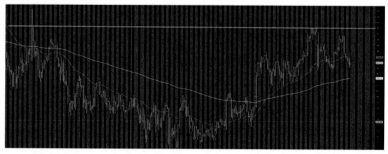

The yellow line at 192 toward the top of the chart is acting as a hard support line on the 4h time frame for $HD.

Trendlines are very similar to support and resistance. In fact, trendlines can be support or resistance lines—they are just drawn on the chart differently. A trendline is a line drawn over pivot points on a chart.

Trendlines are shown on this $MSFT chart in blue.
Both are individual trendlines, the upper indicating resistance and the lower indicating support.

Trendlines give a visual representation of support and resistance, and give investors and traders an idea of what price action is currently doing (and what it may do) for a particular stock. To create a trendline as shown in the above graphic, we look at any time frame chart and connect the high or low points. Remember, they do not have to be exact—the primary intent is to paint a picture of what is happening with price action.

Key levels: Premarket

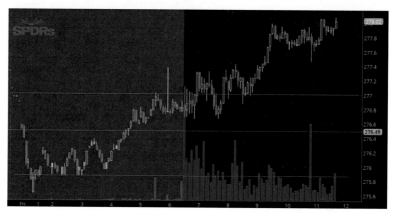

This screen shows premarket key levels on $SPY (5m chart).

Key levels is just another way to refer to support and resistance lines. In the above graphic, we can see that in the first few hours of trading, price action respected the key level at 277 that was set in the premarket trading session. Throughout your analysis, you will find that key levels from premarket trading are often respected throughout the trading session. They can provide great entry and exit for your positions and give additional insight into what price action for a particular stock may do next.

Whole and half dollar marks

You will often see support and resistance at whole or half dollar marks (depending on the price of the underlying— over $100 is usually whole dollar, under $100 could be at half dollar). This knowledge is especially useful when a stock is reaching all-time highs (ATHs) and you don't know when to take profits, or if you're in the midst of a trade and don't necessarily have time to look back and see where strong support/resistance is. If I am holding a trade that is doing well and running, I will generally at least take some profit off the table and lock it in (closing part of the trade) at whole or half dollar marks. This is a great tactic and will really assist you in your risk management procedures.

BULLISH & BEARISH FLAG PATTERNS & WEDGES

These technical analysis techniques are some of my absolute favorites. They are simple and have shown success in trading time and time again. These patterns are easy to recognize, and in my opinion, are some of the most textbook setups you can find on a daily basis, no matter the time frame you are choosing to analyze.

Ascending triangle and bullish flag

The ascending triangle is formed with a hard resistance line and an ascending trendline following price action toward the resistance line. As the triangle tightens and price action pushes deeper into the wedge, you can usually expect a "snap" to the upside. Here is an example:

This ascending triangle is formed by a yellow resistance line (at 60) and a yellow trendline on $MU 5m chart.

As you can see, we have a firm resistance that has formed on the 5m $MU chart. Price action followed the trendline leading up to the resistance line. As it got tighter within the wedge (triangle), you can see the exact moment at which it snapped higher. The last few candles before the inevitable breakout (above the yellow line), appear to be trading in a very tight range. This type of action is often referred to as coiling. Recognizing when a stock is coiling (no matter the time frame) can be beneficial to a trader.

> *Coiling price action can be thought of as a spring: The tighter it coils into the wedge, the more explosive the snap will be when it finally breaks.*

Very similar to an ascending triangle is the bullish flag pattern. The key difference between the two is that the bull flag has a sharp movement upward forming the "flag pole".

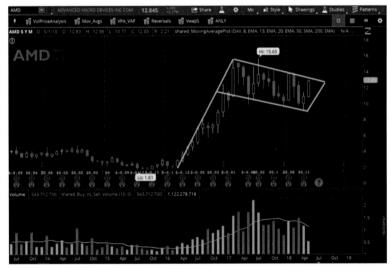

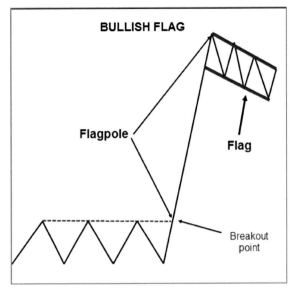

Bull flag on the $AMD 5-year 1-month chart. This is a very big time frame, so the expected "snap" will likely be a very large move.

After the pole has formed, consolidation in price action follows, which creates the flaglike shape. When the breakout occurs and the upper line of the flag is finally broken (similar to the ascending triangle), a snap upward can be expected.

Descending triangle and bearish flag

Both of these bearish patterns are extremely similar to their bullish counterpart, just inversed.

The descending triangle is formed with a support line and a resistance trendline that is following price action toward the support level. Remember that all of these patterns are only guidelines, and you will seldom find any single example that is perfect. It is the general principle and idea that we are looking for when conducting the analysis.

In this descending triangle example ($ULTA 1d 5m chart), the red line indicates support level (which was broken); the yellow and teal trendlines indicate two ways a trendline can be visualized.

In the example, we had a nice firm support level just shy of 253. This support level was also apparent in the preceding trading days. Price action bounced off this level right at the market open (as indicated by the first candle), lost its strength, and then slowly found its way back to the support level. When this level was lost, we see that a sharp move down took place. In this particular example, purchasing weekly expiring ATM (at the money) puts would have seen a very nice return on investment within 15 to 20 minutes!

Similar to the descending triangle is the bear flag pattern. The bear flag is exactly the same as the bull flag, but the pattern is inverted. With the bear flag, setup of the pattern first begins with a sharp move downward. This is followed by consolidation, which would form the flag.

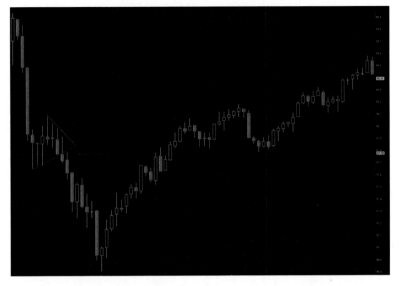

Looking at this $MSFT 1d 5m chart, we can see that the day opened with some selling, which was followed by consolidation and then another move downward. This makes our bearish flag pattern.

When it comes to taking entry and establishing position on any of the bullish or bearish patterns discussed in this chapter, it is important to enter only when your analysis is confirmed. Any entry prior to confirmation would be speculative. If you do decide to take a speculative (early) entry, it would be wise to go into this trade with "half size," meaning that if you normally do $1000 per trade, you should do only $500 on this particular trade. Remember that speculative entries will only increase your risk!

Additionally, TA-charting purists would likely consider what I call a flag to be a pennant. See the next figure for details on the discrepancies. While there is a very slight difference, such minute details will not make a significant difference in your trading. The important thing to recognize is the pattern itself: With both the flag and the pennant we have a sharp move followed by a period of consolidation. This alone identifies the continuation pattern.

Flags and Pennants

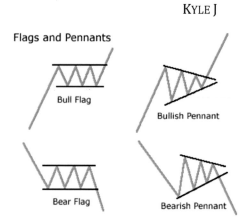

There are slight variations between
bullish and bearish flags and pennants.

BULLISH & BEARISH REVERSAL CANDLES

Reversal candles reveal a change in the direction of a price trend, which can be a positive or negative change. Seeing a reversal is beneficial to us as traders because it can potentially provide a great point of entry for a trade. Reversals are a recognizable change, and they are oftentimes preceded by a particular type of candle. It is important to note that there are hundreds of identifiable reversal candle setups, but I don't find it necessary to use or even know them all. So, I will go over my favorites and the ones I use on a regular basis to assist with my analysis.

Additionally, reversal candles paired with support and resistance lines are an even better way to confirm whether your analysis is correct. Remember that each of these chapters offers a tool to identify what is happening with price action. Used in conjunction with one another, they increase your chances of being correct with your analysis and thus profitable with your trades.

Bullish reversal candles

Bullish reversal candles are seen at the bottom of a downtrend. They indicate that a stock is about to go up. One of the most consistent and reliable bullish reversal candles is known as the hammer candle.

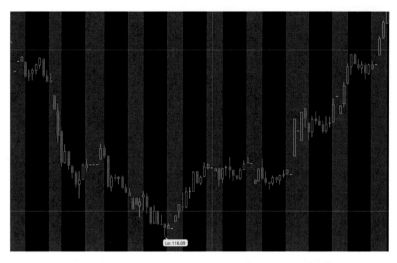

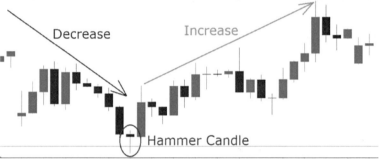

These screens show two examples of bullish hammer candles, indicating the end of a downtrend and the beginning of a bullish trend.

The hammer candle indicates that buyers are stepping in at that price level. This can be a great entry point for calls. That being said, I would always recommend waiting for confirmation that the trend is changing before entering in. While you may lose a couple percentage points of profit, you still get the meat of the move with less risk! Key features to note on a hammer candle include: short body, long bottom tail (preferably the tail is at least double the size of the body); no wick (aka upper shadow or tail); and formation on a key level or support zone. Ideally the hammer candle should be green.

That brings us to the bullish engulfing candle, which requires looking at two candles. The key features are as follows: The first candle shows up during a downtrend and will ideally be a small-body red candle. The candle following this one is green, and the body of this second candle FULLY engulfs the entirety of the previous candle, wick and tail included.

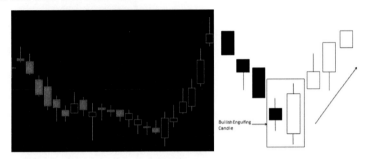

Notice the size of the second candle
in these examples of bullish engulfing patterns.

Again, like the hammer candle, the bullish engulfing candle is most effective at a key level or area of support.

Doji setups

Next, we have the morning star doji candle setup. Much like the bullish engulfing pattern, this setup requires two candles. The first is interrupted by a doji (which looks like two crossed lines). Following the doji, there is a green candle, which ideally closes higher than the doji.

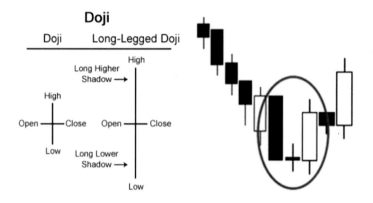

On the left are general doji and how to read them. Notice how small the body of the candle is—it's nearly nonexistent.
On the right we see an example of the morning star doji.

A doji candle indicates indecision. As seen in the example above, the green (hollow) candle following the doji not only closes higher than the doji, it also closes higher than the midpoint of the red candle preceding the doji. This scenario is not required, but it reinforces our reversal analysis. Just as with the bullish reversal pattern, this reversal can be a great place to enter calls, and proves to be even stronger if it takes place on a key area of support.

Dojis overall are one of my favorite candles to use for identifying a reversal. They can appear as both bullish and bearish reversals: The inverse of all three of the patterns shown can signal bearish reversals. As with the bullish and bearish flag patterns, we simply "flip" the chart to see bullish candlestick reversal patterns as bearish reversal indicators!

Allow me to illustrate with some examples:

Shooting Star

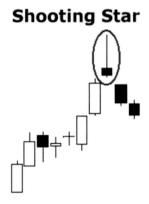

Notice how this shooting star candle basically looks like the hammer candle previously discussed? The shooting star is merely the inverse of the hammer and signals a bearish reversal, as opposed to the bullish reversal of the hammer candle.

Bearish engulfing candle

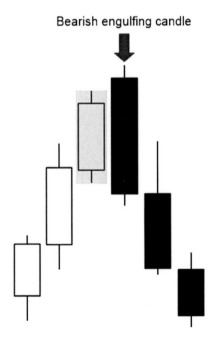

Here we have the bearish engulfing candle. Notice how this particular setup looks almost identical to the bullish engulfing candle, but inversed.

See the similarities? Bullish and bearish patterns are nearly identical—they are merely inversed from each other. This holds true for much of technical analysis. The pattern identification that works for bullish moves also works for bearish moves.

To reiterate, none of the candle setups you see will be textbook examples 100% of the time. The idea is to recognize what is happening with price action, whether the pattern is perfect or not, to help you understand and perhaps identify what might happen next. There are many people out there who look for perfect examples in their technical analysis—these types seldom make consistent profits.

Don't forget that candlestick reversal patterns are best when they take place near an area of support or resistance. Lastly, there are literally hundreds of reversal patterns to find, memorize, and use in your analysis. I suggest finding a few you like that you see often, sticking with them, and mastering them. Trying to learn every single candlestick reversal pattern out there is only going to give you analysis paralysis.

SECTOR PLAYS & SECTOR ROTATION

What are they?

A sector is defined as a group of stocks in the same industry or related industries (i.e., tech: $AAPL, $GOOG, $FB). These stocks will usually have very similar charts. While this is not always the case in everyday examples, the patterns can serve as guidelines.

Sector rotation and sector plays

There are some very important takeaways from sector rotation and sector-based trades that can benefit you when conducting your analysis and scanning for potential trades. For example, if an entire sector is moving up, and one or two stocks within the sector are not following the upward trend, what do you think this indicates? It indicates there is a problem with those particular stocks. A savvy trader can usually take advantage of this depending on which way the move is going. Before blindly placing a trade in this kind of scenario, you would want to identify exactly why this particular stock is experiencing an abnormality and is not following the trend of the rest of the sector.

Money is always rotating and flowing between different sectors. One day might see large inflows of money into the tech sector, and the next day may see money rotating out of tech and into retail. It is important to be conscious of "where the money is" daily. Analyzing premarket moves in price can be a great way to see where money is likely to flow that day. Did $AAPL-$FB-$GOOG gap up in premarket trading from the prior day? Money is likely flowing into tech. Did $HD-$LOW-$NKE gap up in premarket trading from the previous day? Then money is likely flowing into the retail sector. Identifying this kind of action and its meaning can help you succeed with your trades.

Sector plays (aka, sector trades) can be great when you identify an ideal move or are anticipating a move within one stock but aren't quite ready to trade it. For example, you don't like the company, IV was too high for your liking, or there just wasn't enough volume on the particular contracts you were looking to purchase. You can still receive some exposure to the move you're anticipating by trading another similar stock within the same sector.

As an example, let's say you see news that Warren Buffett purchased $10 million worth of $HD (Home Depot), and this caused the option premium to spike. Instead of purchasing $HD, you decide to purchase $LOW (Lowe's) to capture some of the upward momentum in the sector. Remember, whatever stock you are looking to trade, there will almost always be something moving in conjunction with it.

OPTIONS TRADING STRATEGIES

There are a large number of option-specific strategies that you can deploy to turn a profit on the stock market. In this chapter you will find some of my favorites, and while I will give a brief description of each, it would be impossible to cover all of the nuances associated with every strategy. Some of these are wildly popular, and others I have developed on my own. Following this book, if you find yourself curious and wanting to learn more about my strategies, the *Opinicus Holdings Options Mastery Course* covers them all in explicit detail using videos and live examples. You can find details on that course at https://opinicusholdings.com. Remember, no matter the strategy, the backbone of any successful trader is their ability to control their emotion and stick to their risk management plan and trading plan.

Additionally, take every strategy you read and hear about with a grain of salt (including the ones in this book!). Do you know the person who is teaching the strategy? Are they credible and profitable? Will that particular strategy fit your own personal risk management style? Will that strategy fit your time frame? These are all questions to consider when exploring new strategies. As I mentioned in the introduction, it seems like there are more frauds overcharging for their services to make a living than those whose primary income is trading and who offer their services on the side to help others.

The best approach is to absorb as much as you can about a variety of strategies, try out a few, find the ones you like, and refine them. You will gain increasing success in this method of personal research and refinement, until eventually you become so experienced you can truly create something of your own.

Covered calls

This strategy should be used when you are long on the underlying stock (meaning you have purchased and are holding shares), and you think the stock may dip in the short term. This strategy does require owning at least 100 shares, and you would be selling 1 call option contract for every 100 shares you own; i.e., if you own 1000 shares, you would sell 10 calls with this strategy. The purpose of this is to provide a hedge against your shares from the expected dip.

How it works:

1. Conduct TA to determine and confirm that the stock will dip.
2. Create your plan.
3. Sell an OTM call option of whichever expiry you choose (OTM will be safer than ATM).
4. When the underlying stock dips in price, the contract price will also lose value.
5. At this point you can purchase the contracts back at the lower price and receive the credit, or you can elect to let the contracts expire worthless.
6. The profit is credited to your account.

This strategy is ideal if you have a large account or if you already own hundreds of common shares of a particular company.

Straddle

Use this strategy when you expect a large move of the underlying but are unsure of the direction. The setup is very simple: Calls and puts (same quantity for each) of the same strike and the same expiry are purchased ATM. This strategy is designed for wild swings in either direction, which usually happen around major events or announcements, such as an earnings report, news event, geopolitical event, or Federal Reserve meetings and announcements.

Morning momentum

This is a unique strategy that can be quite risky if you are inexperienced, so I highly recommend studying the price action of the first 30 minutes of any given stock to see how it affects the contract prices. This is a great strategy for paper trading prior to using real money. This particular technique is what originally got me so interested in options trading, and what eventually pushed me to quit my job and trade full time.

How it works:

- You first need to search for gappers—stocks that have gapped up or down from the previous day.
- Use the 1m or 2m chart.
- As mentioned, you want to be very cautious with the bid/ask spread on the particular options contract.
  - Have patience: Wait for the B/A spread to tighten before entering.
- Watch how price action reacts around the pre-market key levels, support/resistance, and whole/half dollar marks.

- o If you've purchased a call position and the underlying moves against you, exit the position immediately if a key level is lost.
- o Same is true for upside: If your direction was correct, take profits off at whole/half dollar areas or resistance.

This strategy holds massive profit potential due to the volatility usually seen within the first hour of market open.

In conclusion...

There are a dozen other very useful strategies taught in the *Opinicus Holdings Options Mastery Course* via video lessons. Unfortunately, the depth of explanation and examples required does not make them appropriate to discuss in book form. Our Fast/Slow Crossover, BB Widening, and 5MSR are all superior strategies that can be used every single day to produce profit. That being said, learning our ways is not required to make a profit with options. There are hundreds of strategies out there; we just choose to promote a variety of tested and proven ways that can be used day in and day out. At the end of the day, what matters is usability and fit for you as a trader.

INDICATORS

Indicators and studies: What are they?

Indicators, sometimes referred to as studies, are advanced calculations based on a variety of inputs from price, volume, or open interest of an underlying stock. People often believe that by analyzing the history of price action, they can get a good indication of what might be in store for the future. However, more often than not people rely too heavily on indicators to dictate their trading. Indicators should always be used as a helping hand in your analysis, trading, and scalping and not as a rule!

There are two types of indicators: overlays and oscillators. Overlays quite literally overlay the price action on the chart. Oscillators move between minimum and maximum values and are usually plotted below the chart.

Indicators are another way for traders to get the dreaded analysis paralysis. Personally, I occasionally use relative strength index, volume-weighted average price, moving averages, and a money flow oscillator—the basics of these will be discussed below. While I do find that these are useful tools, I always come back to what is absolute—and what's absolute is price. As you are likely starting to gather, I am a huge proponent of a "less is more" approach when it comes to trading. Why cloud your judgment and potentially cause yourself to second-guess with messy indicators? There is a time and place for everything, but in my experience in the day trading arena and in coaching and educating others, students and amateurs are overusing indicators. As we go through the various indicators listed, keep in mind that I do not view them all simultaneously. Each paints its own picture of what is happening with the price, so I prefer to view them individually in most cases.

Relative strength index (RSI)

RSI is an oscillator indicator that is based on momentum. It is perhaps one of the most popular indicators used today and compares the size of recent gains and losses over a designated period of time to calculate speed (and change) of price in the underlying security. If this sounds complex, it's because it is. What you really need to know about RSI is that it can indicate when a stock is over-bought or oversold.

As previously mentioned, oscillator-style indicators move between minimum and maximum values, in this case (and in most cases) it is between 0 and 100. Conventional RSI wisdom says that values above 70 indicate overbought and values below 30 indicate oversold.

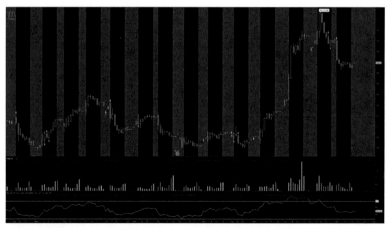

$MCD 1h chart with RSI shown at the very bottom. We see the silver oscillator line turn red when it crosses above the tan line at the 75 level, indicating that it was overbought.

I prefer to set RSI overbought and oversold values at 75 and 25, respectively. This gives an even stronger indication of whether a stock is overbought or oversold. RSI works on any time frame that you choose. The indicator's standard settings will be 14, 70, 30, which means its movement is based on 14 trading periods and uses the conventional 70/30 levels of bought and sold. The 14 would mean 14 trading days if using a daily chart, but if you are using an hourly, 5m, 1m or any other time frame, the period is based on the most recent 14 candlesticks.

Volume weighted average price (VWAP)

VWAP is used by institutional traders as well as algorithmic traders. It is very similar to moving averages (MAs) in that it is an overlay indicator and tracks similarly to MAs, but it can be more useful than MAs because it takes volume into consideration.

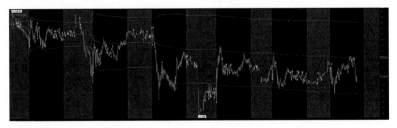

VWAP shown on the $NVDA 5m chart. You can clearly see how price action moves between the purple lines.

VWAP can be a great indicator for support and resistance when a stock is reaching all-time highs or if you are presently in a trade and don't have time to look back at the chart. Notice above in the $NVDA example (5m chart) how the stock seems to move between the midline and the lower line. This is not a coincidence.

On the VWAP indicator, the middle line represents the actual volume weighted average price, while the upper and lower lines are +2 or -2 (for upper and lower, respectively), standard deviations from the midline. Load this indicator on various charts of various time frames and see just how useful it is. We have a strategy in the *Opinicus Holdings Options Master Course* that is built around VWAP entirely!

Moving Averages (MAs)

MAs are likely the most popular indicator out there. Like all indicators, they have a time and place and can be useful in your analysis, but far too many people rely too heavily on them.

What are MAs? Moving averages help to identify trends in the price action by showing a smoothed-out line mimicking the action. MAs filter out the noise and give a simplified idea of what the price is doing. MAs are both an overlay indicator and a lagging indicator, the latter because they are derived from past price performance.

How do they work? Moving averages take the average of the period you select and overlay a line on the chart for that period. For example, if you were looking at the 12MA on a daily chart, the MA would be calculating the previous 12 days' average price and overlaying the indicator on your chart, with each candle representing 1 day; if it were a 5m or 1h chart, it would be calculating the 12 most recent candles.

The orange line in this $MA 1d chart is a 48MA.

In the graphic above, we can see a 48MA. Notice how it kind of "guides" the price action and resembles a trendline. For this reason, MAs are very informative when used in conjunction with your overall technical analysis. My personal favorite periods to follow are 8, 12, 50, and 200 days.

In closing...

If you are new to indicators, use them sparingly and do your absolute best not to rely on them too heavily. Remember, they are a helping hand, not an absolute! You want to avoid analysis paralysis at all costs. It is best to try to get a grasp of what is happening with price action without having to use indicators at all. The more complex you make things, the harder it will be for you to be successful. Keeping things simple works in both life and in technical analysis!

QUAD WITCHING AND LOW-VOLUME FRIDAYS

Quad Witching

Quad witching (aka quadruple witching) is very important for options traders to be aware of. Even many seasoned traders have no idea what quad witching is or when it occurs. Quad witching happens four times a year, in the third week of March, June, September, and December. It refers to the expiration date of four individual asset classes: index futures, stock index options, stock options, and single stock futures. This results in a volume spike and volatile price changes in both underlying shares as well as the options contract prices.

This volatility is a result of institutional traders rolling out their contracts to a farther expiry or selling altogether. Regardless, keep these dates marked on your calendar. There is a much higher risk involved in trading on these days, and I would highly recommend avoiding them.

Low-volume Friday

This is rather self-explanatory: Generally speaking, Fridays will experience lower volume and more docile behavior in the market. Of course this is a generalization and will not hold true for every stock on every Friday. I seldom trade on Fridays, as the moves are usually lackluster and thus do not interest me as a day trader. If you must, I suggest keeping all trades light—as in half-size—and taking profit quickly.

DEFENSIVE EXITING

Defensive exiting is an advanced risk management strategy. It is more of a mentality than anything actionable. If you are new to trading, I do not recommend this approach to exiting positions unless it is absolutely necessary.

We are going to discuss the unfortunate but inevitable here. Let's start with a hypothetical trade situation (if this has not happened to you yet, it will at some point): Your trade goes against you and is approaching your stop-loss or mental stop-loss; remember, a mental stop-loss is an area or zone where you know you will cut the trade but do not have an explicit order in, to allow the trade some wiggle room. You have already conducted your analysis and have your trade plan in place. You have your trendlines and support/resistance lines drawn on the chart. At this point the price action is moving quickly against you, and you have exceeded the maximum loss you were willing to accept per your trade plan and risk management procedure.

What to do now? In this situation, most folks will do one of two things: panic sell or panic buy. They let emotion totally take control of their thought process and make a rash decision. I have seen this happen in my own early trading behavior, as well as in the behavior of my freshly oriented students. The most important action is to remain level headed! Act swiftly but do not do anything out of impulse. Create a backup plan for how you will manage this type of trade. Often in a situation like this, I will allow the price to move to a key area, and at this point I will be ready to pounce and double down on the position. Double down here refers to dollar amount, not the number of contracts—for example, a $100 initial trade would be a $200 double down.

Of course, this violates everything that was suggested in the risk management chapter. For that reason, this strategy should be attempted only by those who have adequate experience with options and who keep their emotions (when trading) in check. Following the double down, when the price action effectively bounces, you'll scale your position back to a reasonable dollar amount, as you see fit. I have been in many situations where I used this last line of defense with a trade and have come out at break even, and even occasionally with profit!

This line of defense highlights why it is so important to keep "dry powder" (cash) available. Not only does opportunity present itself when you least expect it, but sometimes your position runs hard against you before you can act.

CLOSING STATEMENTS

In this profession, you are not paid by the number of hours you put in. Your perseverance, mental strength, and ability to suppress emotion will determine your success in this game. Learning the markets and your own capacity for discipline requires an enormous amount of work. Once learned, you will be able to do what most people cannot: Achieve financial freedom. It is possible for anyone. You do not need to possess certain character traits to be successful in this arena. Becoming a profitable trader, whether trading full time or not, is entirely possible for anyone willing to put in the late hours required to master this craft.

On that note, completing your research and analysis the night prior to your trading day will be immensely helpful to achieving success. Follow up with your premarket analysis, and you'll find yourself more than ready when the opening bell rings and your broker platform comes alive.

Additionally, when it comes time to enter your trade, remember to always have a plan. Don't just look at a chart and think you have a plan. Formulate an exact, actionable plan for the trade. If you cannot complete this step, you simply should not enter the trade! If needed, discuss your trade ideas with members in the Opinicus Thinktank— this can be immensely helpful to ironing out any kinks in your plan, as another set of eyes on the same chart is always beneficial.

After your trade plan is complete and you have executed the trade, remember your rules and stick to them! The problem that almost every trader has on down days is that they don't trade their knowledge, they trade their feelings. For example, if you were bullish when $AAPL was 160, why did that change when the price hit 155? It should have made you even more bullish. Your mentality should not change! People too often second guess their plays. Yes, options have a time decay component and you have to limit your losses due to this component. But you should always have a plan, and if that plan fails, you should have a contingency plan! In the military, they use PACE: primary, alternate, contingency, and emergency planning. This type of preparation separates the many from the few.

Options are your vehicle. You need that vehicle to be as efficient as possible if this is your profession. Your vehicle must have small spreads and great liquidity. For example, $AAPL: Very few other tickers come close, let alone parallel, the market like this one (or $SPY, for example) so why put yourself at a huge disadvantage to begin with? Invest in many stocks, but trade in few. This isn't darts—trading is a business. You cannot trade as your profession and treat it like a game. While it is fun to play the high flyers, you need to have your reliable plays to survive.

Made in the USA
San Bernardino, CA
09 December 2018